西安交通大学"十四五"规划教材
西安交通大学少年班规划教材 · 英语

U0743234

# BRIDGE TO COLLEGE

## 交流与表达(4)

COMMUNICATION FOR ACADEMIC STUDY

牛莉◎总主编

龚颖 成旻◎本册主编

西安交通大学出版社
XI'AN JIAOTONG UNIVERSITY PRESS

国家一级出版社
全国百佳图书出版单位

**图书在版编目(CIP)数据**

交流与表达.4：英文 / 牛莉总主编；龚颖，成旻
本册主编 . —西安：西安交通大学出版社，2023.1
ISBN 978-7-5693-2775-5

Ⅰ.①交… Ⅱ.①牛… ②龚… ③成… Ⅲ.①英语-
口语-高等学校-教材 Ⅳ.①H319.9

中国版本图书馆 CIP 数据核字(2022)第 170067 号

| 书　　　名 | 交流与表达(4) |
| --- | --- |
| 总 主 编 | 牛　莉 |
| 本 册 主 编 | 龚　颖　成　旻 |
| 责 任 编 辑 | 牛瑞鑫 |
| 责 任 校 对 | 庞钧颖 |

| | |
| --- | --- |
| 出版发行 | 西安交通大学出版社 |
| | (西安市兴庆南路 1 号　邮政编码 710048) |
| 网　　址 | http://www.xjtupress.com |
| 电　　话 | (029)82668357　82667874(市场营销中心) |
| | (029)82668315(总编办) |
| 传　　真 | (029)82668280 |
| 印　　刷 | 西安五星印刷有限公司 |

| | | | | | |
| --- | --- | --- | --- | --- | --- |
| 开　　本 | 787 mm×1092 mm　1/16 | 印张 | 3.75 | 字数 | 76.2 千字 |
| 版次印次 | 2023 年 1 月第 1 版　　2023 年 1 月第 1 次印刷 | | | | |
| 书　　号 | ISBN 978-7-5693-2775-5 | | | | |
| 定　　价 | 36.00 元 | | | | |

如发现印装质量问题，请与本社市场营销中心联系。
订购热线：(029)82665248

# 总序
## Foreword

　　1985 年对西安交通大学来说是值得铭记的年份。这一年,教育部正式批准学校开办少年班,学校积极贯彻邓小平同志的指示:"在人才的问题上,要特别强调一下,必须打破常规去发现、选拔和培养杰出的人才。"转眼间,少年班已走过了三十五年的办学历程,在破解"如何发现智力超常少年并因材施教"这一极具挑战性的难题上,西安交通大学先后的五位校长,艰难探索,矢志不渝,构建了一套适合中国国情且自主创新的少年班人才选拔和培养体系,培养了一批又一批少年英才。目前,少年班从初中应届毕业生中选拔招生,实行"预科—本科—硕士"的八年制贯通培养模式,其中,预科一年级在指定的四所优秀预科中学学习,预科二年级在大学学习,为期各一年。

　　如何实现基础教育与高等教育的有机衔接一直是少年班探索和研究的重点,而教材作为知识衔接的重要载体,成为影响少年班教育质量的关键因素。为此,钱学森学院于 2010 年 10 月成立少年班教材编写小组,正式启动教材编写研究工作。全国首套少年班系列教材出版于 2014 年 12 月。来自大学及高中的近 60 名专家和一线教师参与其中,谨遵"因材施教、发掘潜能、注重创新、超常教育、培养英才"的指导思想,通过多次研讨、仔细斟酌、反复修订和严格审核,耗时四年有余,最终编写并出版了全国首套将"预科—本科"有机衔接的教材。这套教材包含六门课程,共 22 册,总计 2550 学时,828 万字。这套教材自出版至今,使用效果良好。

　　2018 年,经过大量调研,钱学森学院制定了新版少年班培养方案,在新版培养方案的基础上规划修订数学、物理、化学、英语等课程的教材,并于 2020 年启动少年班"十四五"规划教材的编写和出版工作。此版教材将力求实现"预科—本科"课程的无缝衔接,从知识体系、内容结构、案例设计、习题配套等方面对教材内涵和风格进行重新编撰和优化,同时注重拔尖学生的发展需求,体现新版少年班培养方案中"以兴趣为导向"的教育教学改革思想。

　　愿此版教材可让更多关注少年班的有识之士受益。同时,我们也希望借此机会,号召大家集思广益,群策群力,共同为推动少年英才培养进程做出努力。

　　是为序。

杨　森

2020 年 8 月 10 日

从 2012 年接手少年班的教学工作开始,我们的教学团队一直在探索适合少年班的英语教学模式,包括课程设置、教学内容、教学方法与手段、评价方式及教材等。2018 年我校钱学森学院重新制定了少年班培养方案,我们团队也借此机会对我们的教学模式重新进行了梳理,决定开设两门英语课程:"阅读与写作(Reading and Writing for Academic Study)"和"交流与表达(Communication for Academic Study)"。因此,为这两门课程而编写的两套同名教材应运而生。同时,基于少年班英语课程培养方案的总目标,即"帮助学生完成从通用英语(English for General Purpose, EGP)到学业英语(English for Academic Study, EAS)的过渡,为学生进入大学学习做好语言能力的准备",我们又将这两套教材的编写内容进行了有机结合,构成了"通往大学"系列(*Bridge to College*)。

本系列教材有三个特色:

一、教材编写突出体现"以学习为中心"和"以成果为导向"的教学理念,如下图所示:

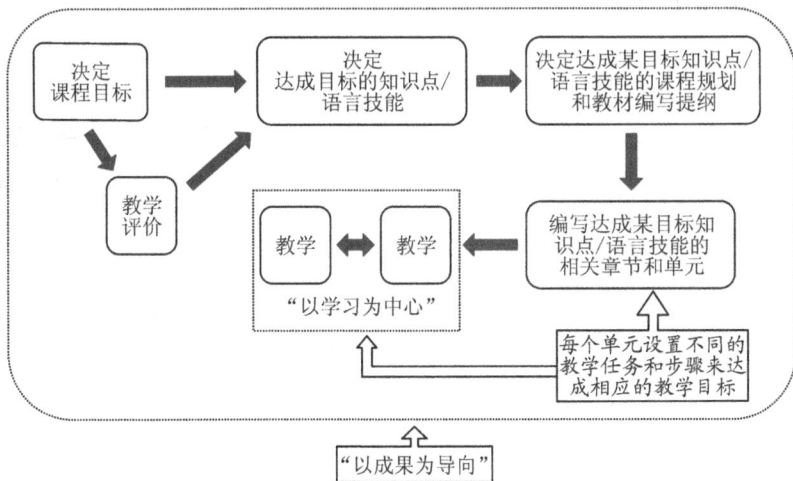

二、教材章节编排侧重构建英语语言知识和技能体系。与一般英语教材中以话题为章节(theme-based)的编写原则不同,本教材采用以功能编写各章节(function-based,即突出对语言知识点和技能的培养)的编写原则。因为,以话

题为章节的编写理念侧重扩充相关话题的词汇量或表达,忽视了语言知识点或语言技能之间的相关性,缺乏系统性,会导致学生在学习之后只能想起某些课文的内容;而本教材以功能为章节进行编写,其目的在于帮助学生获得相关知识点或技能,同时也帮助学生构建出完整的英语语言知识和技能体系。

三、教材内容融入教学设计。本教材中的各章节内容,不仅是学生应掌握的相关知识点,同时也是教师在教学中的具体目标。本教材的章节编排突破了传统英语教材"课文+练习"的模式,变为"通过设置不同的教学任务和步骤来达成相应的教学目标"的模式。这样的编写模式,既包含了学生学习的过程,也体现了教师教学的过程,实现了"以学习为中心",即"教师为主导,学生为主体"的教学理念。

基于上述编写特点,本系列教材也适用于高中生和本科生自主学习。

最后,特别感谢各位编写老师牺牲难得的假期投入教材编写工作!特别感谢西安交通大学附属中学刘晏辰老师对预科一年级教材讲义初稿的试用和及时的意见反馈!特别感谢少年班 2017 级、2018 级的同学们对教材讲义试用和新教学模式探索的积极配合和肯定!特别感谢西安交通大学钱学森学院和外国语学院给予我们团队的各种支持!特别感谢我们教学团队(包括各中学和大学的所有老师)的辛勤付出!

牛　莉

2020 年暑假

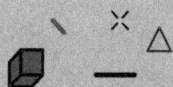

# 目 录
## Table of Contents ▶

# 1

## Project Camping

- Learning to tell Chinese stories
- Doing problem-oriented case study
- Recognizing logical reasoning and logical fallacies
- Coping with academic research

## Project 1
## Learning to Tell Chinese Stories

◈ **Preparation Task**

➲ **Step 1**　Read the questions:

1. How can we express our Chinese culture, that is, how can we tell Chinese stories in international communication?

2. How can we deal with Chinese terms in international communication?
   - Translate or not?
   - How to express them clearly to people from different cultures?

➲ **Step 2**　Individually watch 3 TED videos and think about the questions. Note down your answers.

➲ **Step 3**　Work in your group and discuss your answers.

◈ Training Task: Recounting Chopsticks

⊃ **Step 1**　The whole class will be divided into 4 parts. Each part will do research about information as required below. Every member should have a copy of the research results.

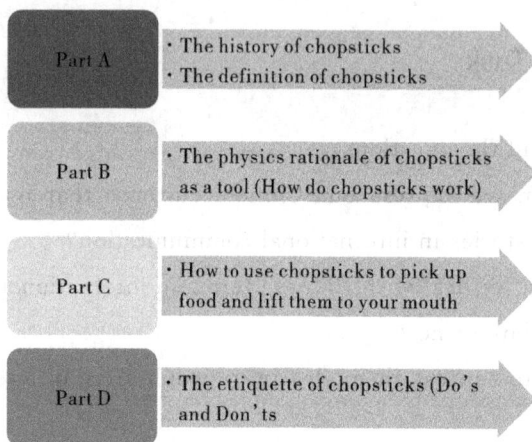

| Part A | · The history of chopsticks<br>· The definition of chopsticks |
|---|---|
| Part B | · The physics rationale of chopsticks as a tool (How do chopsticks work) |
| Part C | · How to use chopsticks to pick up food and lift them to your mouth |
| Part D | · The ettiquette of chopsticks (Do's and Don'ts) |

⊃ **Step 2**　Each part will be numbered from 1 and each person will get his/her number.

⊃ **Step 3**　Move to your new group of the same number. Share your information in turns and take notes.

⊃ **Step 4**　Prepare a group presentation about chopsticks. You may refer to the skills in "Preparing for Presentation" and "Group Presentation" in Presentation Camping, Book 3.

⊃ **Step 5**　Deliver your presentation before your classmates.

◈ Practice Task: Telling the stories of Xi'an Jiaotong University (XJTU)

■ Before-Task Reminders

⮞ **Step 1**   The whole class will be divided into even-numbered groups. Two groups will work together later. The recommended number of people per group is 4 or 5.

⮞ **Step 2**   Read the chart below.

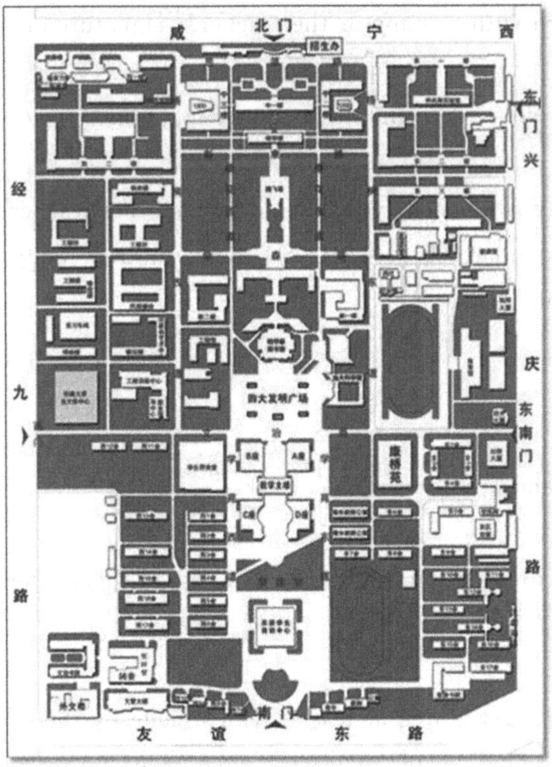

西迁精神路线

**Route of Westward Relocation Spirit**

⬇北门↪

⬇饮水思源碑↪

⬇雪松↪

⬇中心楼↪

⬇杰出校友画廊↪

⬇校风墙↪

⬇西迁广场↪

⬇樱花道↪

⬇梧桐道✪

⬇西花园↪

⬇东花园

⬇腾飞塔广场✪

⬇钱学森图书馆✪

⬇四大发明广场✪

⬇教学主楼✪

⬇思源学生活动中心✪

⬇交大西迁博物馆✪

⬇南门✪

➲ **Step 3**   Prepare your group work.

Suppose your group will be the tourist guides on XJTU campus. The odd groups will be the guides of the sites marked ⚑; the even groups, the sites marked ✪. You are going to tell the stories of the sites. You can do your own research about the information or refer to the book *A Guide to Time Travel*.

➲ **Step 4**   Be ready to video your presentations.

■ In-task reminders

➲ **Step 1**   Start your tour from the North Gate if you are the odd groups or start your tour from the South Gate if you are the even groups. Before your activity, you have to find the teacher at the North Gate or the South Gate and get your postcard with a stamp or the teacher's signature on it.

➲ **Step 2**   Visit each site on your route and do your presentations.

➲ **Step 3**   When your activity is finished, you have to find another teacher at the Four Great Inventions Square（四大发明广场）to get another stamp or teacher's signature on your postcard.

■ Post-task reminders

➲ **Step 1**   Edit your videos and produce a vlog.

➲ **Step 2**   Upload your vlog to an account in Baidu Cloud（百度网盘）offered by your teacher.

➲ **Step 3**   If you are odd groups, watch at least 2 vlogs made by the even groups. If you are even groups, watch at least 2 vlogs made by the odd groups.

➲ **Step 4**　Write comments on 2 vlogs from two aspects: something I can learn and something needed improved. Bring your comments to the next class. This is an individual job.

➲ **Step 5**　Share your comments in your group and do a reflection on this activity and the significance of telling Chinese stories in the international communication. A memo is required.

➲ **Step 6**　Hand in your memo to your teacher.

## Project 2
## Doing Problem-Oriented Case Study

### ◈ Preparation Task

Read the following information about the problem-oriented case study.

---

A successful case study analyses a real-life situation where existing problems need to be solved. It should relate the theory to a practical situation; for example, apply the ideas and knowledge discussed in the coursework to the practical situation at hand in the case study.

1. Identify the problems.

2. Select the major problems in the case.

3. Suggest solutions to these major problems.

4. Recommend the best solution to be implemented.

5. Detail how this solution should be implemented.

(Source:www. monash. edu/rlo/quick-study-guides/writing-a-case-study)

---

◈ Case-Study Task

Read the following instructions and do your case study.

| | |
|---|---|
| 1 | **Purposes of doing case study and grouping**<br><br>• There are 3 – 4 persons in each group.<br>• The groups of odd numbers （G1，3，5 ...）：Case should be on "how to persuade ... to avoid frauds or scams".<br>• The groups of even numbers （G2，4，6 ...）：Case should be on "how to persuade ... not to be deceived by fake news or misinformation". |
| 2 | **Requirements of this task**<br><br>• Your group will have one week to do this case study and prepare for your group presentation on your case study.<br>• Your group presentation will last 10 – 15 minutes.<br>• This presentation will be a PPT presentation and a virtue presentation. （See "Village 6—Presentation Camping".）<br>• Please read "Group Presentation Task" page 11.<br>• After class，do your virtue presentation on Tencent Meeting with another group：<br>G1＋G2<br>G3＋G4<br>G5＋G6<br>G7＋G8<br>G9＋G10<br>• Record your presentations and evaluate the other group's presentation with the rubric offered by your teacher.<br>• Hand in your record and evaluation rubric as required by your teacher. |

| | |
|---|---|
| 3 | **Procedures**<br><br>• Individually search some real-life examples for your analysis (e. g., telecommunication fraud, fake news spread via WeChat, etc.)<br>• Individually do the case analysis according to information offered in Memory Task. Note down your analysis.<br>• Work with your group members: share your analysis and prepare for your group presentation.<br>• Hand in your e-memo to Black Board (思源学堂) before the class is over. |
| 4 | **Friendly reminders**<br><br>• Before discussion, do information searching and analysis on your own. You are so smart that you can well prepare YOUR ideas/contributions/analysis for your group work.<br>• Time for your discussion: at least 30 mins<br>• Working language: English<br>• Play your roles in the discussion and shoulder the responsibilities.<br>• Everyone's idea is equal in your discussion.<br>• Your solutions to the problem(s) in your case should include the answers to the question in the section "Purposes of doing case study", and thus consider the proper use of modes of persuasion should be taken into consideration.<br>• You may have your Tencent Meeting for preparation after the class if necessary. For example, you need at least one meeting to do presentation rehearsal. |

◈ Group Presentation Task

Friendly reminder：Read the chart below carefully to learn how to structure a motivated/persuasive presentation for problem-oriented case study.

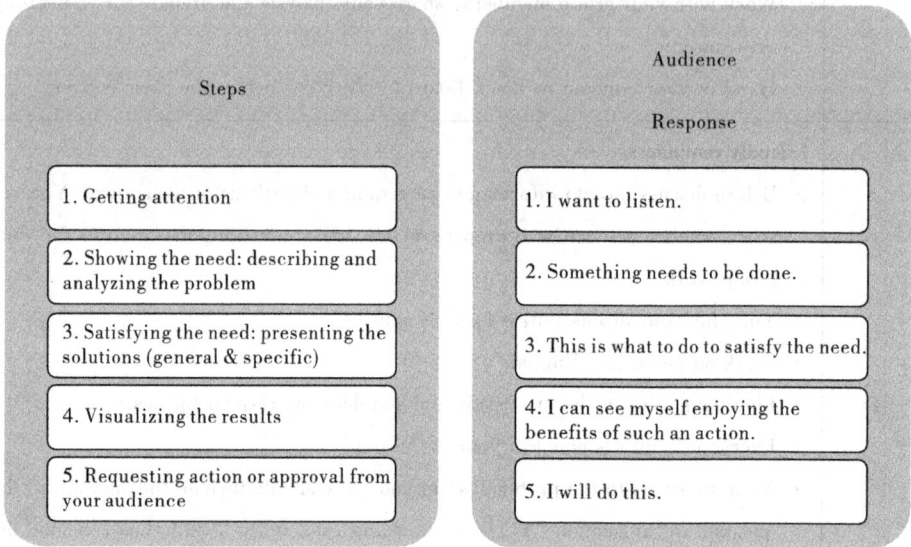

| Steps | Audience Response |
|---|---|
| 1. Getting attention | 1. I want to listen. |
| 2. Showing the need: describing and analyzing the problem | 2. Something needs to be done. |
| 3. Satisfying the need: presenting the solutions (general & specific) | 3. This is what to do to satisfy the need. |
| 4. Visualizing the results | 4. I can see myself enjoying the benefits of such an action. |
| 5. Requesting action or approval from your audience | 5. I will do this. |

## Project 3
## Recognizing Logical Reasoning &
## Common Logical Fallacies

### ◈ Task 1: Learning two ways of logical reasoning

**➲ Step 1**　Read the following information about two ways of logical reasoning.

In order to enhance the ability to effectively communicate an intended message in your extended writing, it's important to understand the concept of logical reasoning, which will direct you to draw a conclusion in your research both valid and sound.

**Reasoning**

Reasoning is the act or process of drawing conclusions from facts or evidences.

Two kinds of logical reasoning can be distinguished. Given a precondition or premise, a conclusion or logical consequence and a rule or material conditional that implies the conclusion given the precondition, one can explain that:

- Deductive reasoning determines whether the truth of a conclusion can be determined for that rule, based solely on the truth of the premises. Example: "When it rains, things outside get wet. The grass is outside, therefore: when it rains, the grass gets wet." Mathematical logic and philosophical logic are commonly associated with this type of reasoning.

- Inductive reasoning attempts to support a determination of the rule. It hypothesizes a rule after numerous examples are taken to be a conclusion that follows from a precondition in terms of such a rule. Example: "The grass got wet numerous times when it rained, therefore: the grass always gets wet when it rains. " While they may be persuasive, these arguments are not deductively valid. Science is associated with this type of reasoning.

(Source: https://en. wikipedia. org/wiki/Logical_reasoning)

**Tips**

1. Deductive reasoning links premises with conclusions.

   An example:

   Premise 1: All men are mortal.

   Premise 2: Socrates is a man.

   Conclusion: Socrates is mortal.

2. Inductive reasoning derives general principles from specific observations.

   An example:

   Premise: 90% of biological life forms that we know of depend on liquid water to exist.

   Conclusion: Therefore, if we discover a new biological life form it will probably depend on liquid water to exist.

   (Source: Desmond Morris, *The Naked Ape*, New York: Dell Publishing Co. Inc. , 1967. )

**Differences Between Deductive Reasoning and Inductive Reasoning**

The differences between deductive reasoning and inductive reasoning are shown in the following table.

| Deductive Reasoning | Inductive Reasoning |
| --- | --- |
| This is based on logic. | This is based on assumption. |
| Numerous premises are logically connected to arrive at a conclusion. | A premise of the sample is taken to arrive at a conclusion about the population. |
| Deductive reasoning is referred to as top-down logic. | Inductive reasoning is a bottom-up approach. |
| Helps in checking a hypothesis, theorem, and confirming with facts. | Takes observations and arrives at a hypothesis or theorem. |

**Types of Deductive Reasoning**

The different types of deductive reasoning are based on the premises and the kind of relationship across the premises. The three different types of deductive reasoning are syllogism, modus ponens, and modus tollens. Let us check in detail about each of the deductive reasoning methods.

*Syllogism*

A syllogism is a common form of deductive reasoning which includes a set of premises followed by a concluding statement. The first premise is a conditional statement, and the second premise is another conditional statement which connects with the conclusion of the first premise. And the summary statement concludes by combining the first part of the first premise with the second part of the second premise.

Premise 1: The numbers which are divisible by 2 are multiples of the number 2.
Premise 2: The multiples of the number 2 are all even numbers.
Conclusion: The numbers which are divisible by 2 are all even numbers.

*Modus Ponens*

This type of deductive reasoning can also be referred to as affirming the antecedent because the first statement is generally a conditional statement. And the second statement merely affirming the first part of the previous statement. Let us look at the below example to clearly understand this concept of modus ponens.

Premise 1: If a number lies between 99 and 999, then it is a three-digit number.
Premise 2: The number N is a number lying between 299 and 399.
Conclusion: Therefore, the number N is a three-digit number.

### *Modus Tollens*

Another important form of deductive reasoning is modus tollens，and it is also referred to as the law of contrapositive. This is also referred as the law of contrapositive，since it is opposite to that of modus ponens. Here the second statement contradicts the first part of the conditional statement.

Premise 1：The numbers 4 and 5 are the factors of 20.

Premise 2：The number X is not a factor of 20.

Conclusion：Therefore，X is neither 4 nor 5.

（Source：https://www.cuemath.com/data/deductive-reasoning/）

## Types of inductive reasoning

There are many different types of inductive reasoning that people use formally or informally，so we'll cover just a few in this article：inductive generalization，statistical generalization，causal reasoning，sign reasoning，analogical reasoning.

Inductive reasoning generalizations can vary from weak to strong，depending on the number and quality of observations and arguments used.

### *Inductive Generalization*

Inductive generalizations use observations about a sample to come to a conclusion about the population it came from.

Inductive generalizations are also called induction by enumeration.

Example：Inductive generalization

The flamingos here are all pink.

All flamingos I've ever seen are pink.

All flamingos must be pink.

Inductive generalizations are evaluated using several criteria.

Large sample: Your sample should be large for a solid set of observations.

Random sampling: Probability sampling methods let you generalize your findings.

Variety: Your observations should be externally valid.

Counter evidence: Any observations that refute yours falsify your generalization.

### *Statistical Generalization*

Statistical generalizations use specific numbers to make statements about populations, while non-statistical generalizations aren't as specific.

These generalizations are a subtype of inductive generalizations, and they're also called statistical syllogisms.

Here's an example of a statistical generalization contrasted with a non-statistical generalization.

Example: Statistical vs. Non-statistical generalization

| Type of Generalization | Specific Observation | Inductive Generalization |
| --- | --- | --- |
| Statistical | 73% of students from a sample in a local university prefer hybrid learning environments. | Most students from a sample in a local university prefer hybrid learning environments. |
| Non-statistical | 73% of all students in the university prefer hybrid learning environments. | Most students in the university prefer hybrid learning environments. |

### *Causal Reasoning*

Causal reasoning means making cause-and-effect links between different things.

A causal reasoning statement often follows a standard setup:

1. You start with a premise about a correlation (two events that co-occur).

2. You put forward the specific direction of causality or refute any other direction.

3. You conclude with a causal statement about the relationship between two things.

Example: Causal Reasoning

All of my white clothes turn pink when I put a red cloth in the washing machine with them.

My white clothes don't turn pink when I wash them on their own.

Putting colorful clothes with light colors causes the colors to run and stain the light-colored clothes.

Good causal inferences meet a couple of criteria.

Direction: The direction of causality should be clear and unambiguous based on your observations.

Strength: There's ideally a strong relationship between the cause and the effect.

### *Sign Reasoning*

Sign reasoning involves making correlational connections between different things.

Using inductive reasoning, you infer a purely correlational relationship where nothing causes the other thing to occur. Instead, one event may act as a "sign" that another event will occur or is currently occurring.

Example: Sign Reasoning

Every time Punxsutawney Phil casts a shadow on Groundhog Day, winter lasts six more weeks.

Punxsutawney Phil doesn't cause winter to be extended six more weeks.

His shadow is a sign that we'll have six more weeks of wintery weather.

It's best to be careful when making correlational links between variables. Build your argument on strong evidence, and eliminate any confounding variables, or you may be on shaky ground.

### Analogical Reasoning

Analogical reasoning means drawing conclusions about something based on its similarities to another thing. You first link two things together and then conclude that some attribute of one thing must also hold true for the other thing.

Analogical reasoning can be literal (closely similar) or figurative (abstract), but you'll have a much stronger case when you use a literal comparison.

Analogical reasoning is also called comparison reasoning.

Example: Analogical reasoning

Humans and laboratory rats are extremely similar biologically, sharing over 90% of their DNA.

Lab rats show promising results when treated with a new drug for managing Parkinson's disease.

Therefore, humans will also show promising results when treated with the drug.

(Source: https://www. scribbr. com/methodology/inductive-reasoning/)

### Two Ways of Reasoning in Academic Research

In the aspect of academic research, deductive reasoning works from the more general to the more specific. Sometimes this is informally called a "top-down" approach. We might begin with thinking up a theory about our topic of interest. We then narrow that down into more specific hypotheses that we can test.

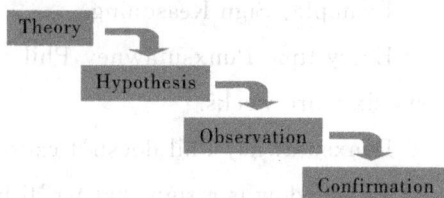

Theory → Hypothesis → Observation → Confirmation

We narrow down even further when we collect observations to address the hypotheses. This ultimately leads us to be able to test the hypotheses with specific data—a confirmation (or not) of our original theories.

In the aspect of academic research, inductive reasoning works the other way, moving from specific observations to broader generalizations and theories. Informally, we sometimes call this a "bottom up" approach. In inductive

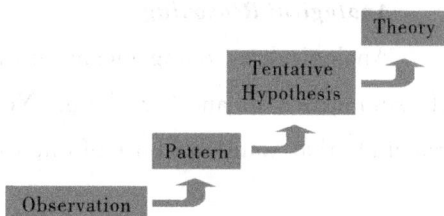

Observation → Pattern → Tentative Hypothesis → Theory

reasoning, we begin with specific observations and measures, begin to detect patterns and regularities, formulate some tentative hypotheses that we can explore, and finally end up developing some general conclusions or theories.

(Source: Desmond Morris, *The Naked Ape*, New York: Dell Publishing Co. Inc., 1967.)

**➥ Step 2**　Read the examples of deductive reasoning and figure out the type of deductive reasoning they belong to.

| Examples | Type |
|---|---|
| 1. In mathematics, If A = B and B = C, then A = C. | |
| 2. Since all humans are mortal, and I am a human, then I am mortal. | |
| 3. All dolphins are mammals; all mammals have kidneys; therefore, all dolphins have kidneys. | |
| 4. Since all squares are rectangles, and all rectangles have four sides, so all squares have four sides. | |
| 5. If Dennis misses work and at work there is a party, then Dennis will miss the party. | |
| 6. All numbers ending in 0 or 5 are divisible by 5. The number 35 ends with a 5, so it is divisible by 5. | |
| 7. To earn a master's degree, a student must have 32 credits. Tim has 40 credits, so Tim will earn a master's degree. | |
| 8. All birds have feathers and robins are birds, so robins have feathers. | |
| 9. It is dangerous to drive on icy streets. The streets are icy now so it is dangerous to drive now. | |
| 10. All cats have a keen sense of smell. Fluffy is a cat, so Fluffy has a keen sense of smell. | |
| 11. Snakes are reptiles and reptiles are cold-blooded; therefore, snakes are cold-blooded. | |
| 12. Cacti are plants and all plants perform photosynthesis; therefore, cacti perform photosynthesis. | |
| 13. Red meat has iron in it and beef is red meat, so beef has iron in it. | |
| 14. Elephants have cells in their bodies and all cells have DNA, so elephants have DNA. | |

➲ **Step 3** Read the following examples of inductive reasoning and figure out the type of inductive reasoning they belong to.

| Examples | Type |
|---|---|
| 1. Jennifer leaves for school at 7:00 a. m. Jennifer is always on time. Jennifer assumes, then, that she will always be on time if she leaves at 7:00 a. m. | |
| 2. The cost of goods was $1.00. The cost of labor to manufacture the time was $0.50. The sales price of the item was $5.00; so, the item always provides a good profit. | |
| 3. Every windstorm in this area comes from the north. I can see a big cloud of dust caused by a windstorm in the distance; so, a new windstorm is coming from the north. | |
| 4. Bob is showing a big diamond ring to his friend Larry. Bob hastold Larry that he is going to marry Joan. Bob has bought the diamond ring to give to Joan. | |
| 5. The chair in the living room is red. The chair in the dining room is red. The chair in the bedroom is red. All chairs in the house are red. | |
| 6. Every time you eat peanuts, your throat swells up and you can't breathe. So, you are allergic to peanuts. | |
| 7. All cats that you have observed purr. Therefore, every cat must purr. | |
| 8. John is an excellent swimmer. John's family has a swimming pool. John's sister Mary must also be an excellent swimmer. | |
| 9. All basketball players in your school are tall, so all basketball players must be tall. | |
| 10. All children in the day care center like to play with Legos. All children, therefore, enjoy playing with Legos. | |
| 11. Ray is a football player. All football players weigh more than 170 pounds. Ray weighs more than 170 pounds. | |
| 12. All observed houses on the South Street are falling apart. Sherry lives on South Street. Her house is falling apart. | |

➲ **Step 4**　Read the following essay and consider the questions below.

1. Can you summarize what you have read into one sentence? Write down your summary.

2. What way(s) of reasoning is/are used in the essay?

### Is There Any Limit for Knowledge?

It is often said that the wish for cognition is one of the most important forces that drive a human being onwards; at least, a human being that has reached certain level of development. It seems that human, if given enough time and power, won't stop until he knows everything that is there to be known. The only thing that separates him from absolute knowledge is the necessity of death; and, as we will show, in more than one sense.

On the one hand, human cannot achieve absolute knowledge for the sheer reason of his life being limited—the information that belongs to collective knowledge of humanity even now exceeds the possibilities of what one man can learn in a lifetime, and the potential knowledge that remains unattainable so far should be of really gargantuan proportions. Yet, we see that people are not confused by the limitedness of the possibilities every separate human has; in their majority people of knowledge are quite satisfied to learn as much as it is possible for them and even more—if they are capable to add something to the existing knowledge.

But, on the other hand, if we consider for a moment a possibility of a human being becoming immortal, will it actually give him an opportunity of attaining complete knowledge? If we take it for granted that the Universe is cognizable, then it will be possible for him in his infinite life to learn everything; but in the end, one final mystery will remain—death. There is no way to learn anything about it by observing it from outside, for in this case we only see it—well, from outside, and perceive only its influence on physical matter.

The one who wants to know everything will finally become exceedingly attracted by death, for it will remain the only unlearnt thing for him. It is often said that great knowledge doesn't bring happiness; in fact, the more person knows, the less happy he is. Isn't it a kind of reverberation of what we have said above? Isn't it this attraction to one final mystery that cannot be learned until you go through it on your own, and once you will, there won't be any possibility for you to impart this knowledge to anyone?

Anyway, as we may see, complete knowledge is impossible for a human being; at least, in the state in which we consider ourselves to be humans.

**○ Step 5** Work in groups of 3 or 4 and discuss the questions in Step 4. Memo is required.

## ◈ Task 2: Recognizing the validity of logical argument

➲ **Step 1**　Read the following information about logical argument.

**Logical Argument**

As defined by logic an argument is simply a sequence of statements in which one statement in the sequence is supported by the other statements in the sequence. The statement that is supported is called the conclusion, and the statements that offer support or reasons in favor of believing the conclusion are called the premises. What is encapsulated in an argument is that reasons are offered in favor of a specific statement. The reasons are contained in the premises.

An argument makes two distinct claims:
- A factual claim—that the premises of the argument are true.
- An inferential claim—that the premises support the conclusion.

Example 1: All tigers are mammals.

No mammals are creatures with scales.

Therefore, no tigers are creatures with scales.

Example 2: All spider monkeys are elephants.

No elephants are animals.

Therefore, no spider monkeys are animals.

In these two examples, the first two sentences in each sequence of sentences is a premise. The premises are offered in favor of the conclusion, which is the final sentence in each sequence.

Arguments occur in a variety of context, and one of the most common contexts they occur in is the natural language of the speaker making the argument. In addition，an argument is offered only when a speaker intends for a set of propositions to support or prove a proposition. This intention is often marked both in speech and writing by the use of inference indicators. Inference indicators are words or phrases that are used to signal the presence of an argument. We use inference indicators to help others recognize when we are giving an argument. There are two kinds ofinference indicators.

| Premise Indicators | Conclusion Indicators |
| --- | --- |
| For | Therefore |
| Since | Thus |
| Because | Hence |
| Seeing that | Assuming that |
| Granted that | For this reason， |
| This is true because | Accordingly， |
| The reason is that | Consequently |
| For the reason that | It follows that |
| In view of the fact that | Which proves that |
| It is a fact that | Which means that |
| Given that | From which we can infer |
| ... | ... |

Premise and conclusion indicators are the main clues for identifying arguments and analyzing their structure. When placed between two sentences to form a compound sentence，a conclusion indicator signals that the first sentence expresses a premise and the second a conclusion from that premise. A premise indicator placed between two sentences to form a compound sentence signals that the first sentence is a conclusion，and that the second sentence is a premise.

For example：
There is no milk in the house，so I need to go to the market.

The conclusion indicator "so" signals "there is no milk in the house" is a premise in support of "I need to go to the market".

A deductive logical argument is one that works from the top to the bottom. It begins with what is known as a "major premise," adds a "minor premise," and attempts to reach a conclusion. A major premise is a statement that names something about a large group, a minor premise takes a single member, and the conclusion attempts to prove that because this single member is a part of the larger group, they must also have the trait named in the original statement.

For example:

MEN ARE TALL: A major premise as it works with a large group of people

BOB IS A MAN: A minor premise as we hear about only one individual of that group

BOB IS TALL: We attempt to make a conclusion based upon what we have already been told

Now, if it is true that men are tall, and that Bob is a man, then we can safely infer that Bob must be tall.

However, beware the logical fallacy. Though it may be true that in certain cultures men are, on average, taller than women, certainly this is not always the case. Being that our major premise is not altogether true, we can now say that this argument is flawed. Furthermore, we might ask what our definition of "tall" is. Tall is different if we are talking about the average population, or basketball players.

An inductive logical argument begins with a firm affirmation of truth, a conclusive statement. By getting the reader to agree with this statement, the argument moves to the next "logical" step. It proceeds in this manner until the argument has led you from one seemingly reasonable conclusion to another that you may not have originally agreed with.

Be aware that there will be logic fallacies hidden in almost every argument. If there is more than one side to an argument, such as in religious or political debates, it is most likely because the argument is impossible to prove. Hence, there will be a logical fallacy present.

### Validity and Soundness of an Argument

In assessing whether a deductive argument is good from a logical point of view there are two criteria the argument must satisfy in order to be good. These criteria are necessary conditions, not sufficient conditions on the goodness of a deductive argument. An argument may satisfy these conditions and still be a bad argument. The two criteria are the following:

- Validity: an argument is valid when it is impossible for the premises to be true, and the conclusion false at the same time.
- Soundness: an argument is sound when it is valid and all of the premises are true.

➲ **Step 2**　Analyze the argument of the essay "Urban Myths or Urban Legends" in our textbook *Reading and Writing for Academic Study* (3) by answering the questions.

1. Is the argument in the essay good?
2. Why or why not?

## ◈ Task 3: Recognizing logical fallacies

➲ **Step 1**   Work in group of 4 persons. Search the information related to the four groups of logical fallacies.

➲ **Step 2**   Get ready for a group presentation to explain the logical fallacies assigned by your teacher. The requirements are as follows:

- Define and exemplify the fallacies with what happens in your daily life in your presentation;
- Each member will be responsible for one part of the speech;
- PPT is needed.

➲ **Step 3**   Individually read the following informal fallacies and try to classify them into categories with your memory and understanding. Then, explain them in Chinese and simple English and provide an example in your daily life for each fallacy. You may search more information about the fallacies on websites or in books.

1. Ad hominem (i. e. personal attack: You attacked your opponent's character or personal traits in an attempt to undermine their argument): Politicians do this frequently (among many logical fallacies, of course).

2. Ambiguity: You used a double meaning or ambiguity of language to mislead or misrepresent the truth.

3. Anecdotal: You used a personal experience or an isolated example instead of a sound argument or compelling evidence.

4. Appeal to authority: You said that because an authority thinks something, therefore it must be true.

5. Appeal to emotion: [= rhetorical ploy ] You attempted to manipulate an emotional response in place of valid or compelling argument.

6. Appeal to nature: You argued that because something is natural, it is valid, justified, inevitable, good, or ideal.

7. Bandwagon (aka. ad populum)：You appealed to popularity or the fact that many people do something as an attempted form of validation.

8. Begging the question：You presented a circular argument in which the conclusion was included in the premise. (Example：The Bible is true because God exists, and God exists because the Bible says so, therefore the Bible is true since God exists ... )

9. Black-or-white (aka. False dilemma, False dichotomy)：You presented two alternative states as the only possibilities, when in fact more possibilities exist (the "grey area")

10. Burden of proof：You said that the burden of proof lies not with the person making the claim, but with someone else to disprove. Extraordinary claims require extraordinary evidence.

11. Composition/Division：［＝invalid references］You assumed that one part of something has to be applied to all, or other, parts of it; or that the whole must apply to its parts.

12. Fallacy fallacy：You presumed that because a claim has been poorly argued, or a fallacy has been made, that the claim itself must be wrong.

13. False cause：You presumed that a real or perceived relationship between things means that one is the cause of the other.

14. Genetic：You judged something as either good or bad on the basis of where it comes from, or from whom it came.

15. Loaded question：You asked a question that had a presumption built into it so that it couldn't be answered without appearing guilty.

16. Middle ground：You claimed that a compromise, or middle point, between two extremes must be the truth.

17. No true Scotsman：You made what could be called an appeal to purity as a way to dismiss relevant criticisms or flows of your argument.

18. Personal incredulity：Because you found something difficult to understand, or areunaware how it works, you made out like it is probably not true. (Example：Donald does not understand how the tides work, and therefore God did it. )

19. Slippery slope: You said that if we allow A to happen, then Z will eventually happen too, therefore A should not happen.

20. Special pleading: You moved the goalposts or made up an exception when your claim was shown to be false.

21. Strawman: Misrepresenting someone's argument to make it easier to attack.

22. Texas sharpshooter: You cherry-picked a data cluster to suit your argument, or found a pattern to fit a presumption. (Example: Climate change deniers zooming in on a small part of the graph and ignoring the trend in the entire data set.)

23. The gambler's fallacy: You said that "runs" occur (like getting 7 red numbers in a row at a roulette table), not realizing that each spin (event) is completely independent.

24. Tu quoque: You avoided having to engage with criticism by turning it back on the accuser. You answered criticism with criticism.

● **Step 4**　Determine what fallacy is committed in the following statements. Maybe there are more than one fallacy in each statement. This is an individual job.

1. Coca-Cola is the best soda in the entire world. This is obvious because everyone drinks it, and the reason they drink it is because it is the best.

2. The past two times I have been to this restaurant; I have had to wait a while to get my food. The management here must not care at all about quality service.

3. I was able to read the book *Where the Wild Things Are* in one weekend. Therefore, I should be able to read the novel *War and Peace* in a weekend as well.

4. There is a lot of social pressure to implement stricter censorship codes on prime-time television these days. But there are actually a lot of good programs on the air at that time. Reality TV shows and the evening news are both on during prime time.

5. The last person to take a shower before the drain started to get backed up was Brian. He must be to blame for clogging it all up.

6. Some people believe that religion should not be taught in elementary schools. But this would amount to firing any teacher who decides to teach religion anyway. Apparently, these people are just hostile towards teachers and want them to lose their jobs. We shouldn't believe them.

7. I overheard some guy on the street saying something about how purified water can cause liver failure. Purified water must be really bad. I'll never drink that stuff again.

8. Some politicians say they are in favor of releasing people from prison who were only convicted of non-violent drug offenses. But if we did that, then there would probably be more politicians arguing for releasing people who have committed armed robbery, followed by a movement to release and rapists and murderers. Pretty soon our streets would be flooded with dangerous people. So, we shouldn't release non-violent drugoffenders.

9. I have seen so many people driving hybrid vehicles lately. They must be really good cars.

10. Either you graduate college or you become a bum for the rest of your life. It's as simple as that.

● **Step 5**　Work in a group of 3 or 4 and discuss your analysis in Step 4.

# Project 4
# Coping with Academic Research

## ◈ Task 1: Learning how to cope with research

**⊃ Step 1**   Before the class, read an excerpt from the book *Study Tasks in English* and do annotated reading about the basic research skills and the language relevant. This is an individual job. Bring your annotation to the class.

**⊃ Step 2**   Finish the Tasks 1.2/1.3/2.4/3 in this excerpt and bring your work to the class. This is an individual job.

**⊃ Step 3**   Work in groups and do the following jobs.

1. Discuss your answers to Tasks 1.2, 1.3, 2.4 and 3. (30 min)
   ☺ Memo is required.
2. Do Tasks 1.4, 2.1, 2.5(c). (30 min)
   ☺ Write down your results or answers on a A3 sheet.
   ☺ This sheet will be used in the poster presentation.
3. Do poster presentation. (20 min)

**⊃ Step 4**   Do after-class task: preparation for your research.

1. Select your research topic:
   ☺ Topics in Task 2.2
   ☺ Or: Any research you have done in the past
   ☺ Or: Any topic you like but not too complex
   ☺ The results of your research should include graph, chart or/and table.

2. Design your research:

- Purpose of your research

- Method(s)

☺ Note down them.

3. Do your research and record the results.

☺ The results of your research should include graph，chart or/and table.

4. Figure out your findings/conclusions of your research.

☺ Note down them.

5. Bring 1，2，3，4 to the next class. Everyone should have a copy of your work.

➲ **Step 5**  Design your research report.

1. Understand the requirements of your research report.

- Type of presentation：group presentation，PPT presentation

- Duration：15 - 20 min

- Language：including accurate use of reporting language and description of graph(s)

2. Discuss your research. Memo is required and should be submitted to your teacher when time is up. （30 min）

☺ Your memo should include the contents：

- Background of your research

- Research topic

- Research question

- Methods

- Results including graphs

- Findings/Conclusions of your research

3. Design your presentation PPT. Hand in your PPT draft to your teacher when the class is over.

⮞ **Step 6**　After class, rehearse your presentation.

☺ After your rehearsal, you can ask the
questions following:

- Is the opening effective?
- Do the transitions work well from
  one idea to the next?
- Do I need to slow my speech rate?
  When? Are some parts better
  faster or slower?
- Do I need pauses? Where? How
  long for?
- Are my words clearly spoken? Can people hear me adequately?
- Are any visual aids I've planned fully integrated into the flow of my
  speech?
- Is the ending strong/suitable and meaningful?
- Does the speech fit the time allowance?

⮞ **Step 7**　Deliver your research report.

☺ During the presentation time, the presentations will be evaluated by
both your teacher and your classmates in other groups with the rubrics

offered by your teacher.

☺ The following are the samples of rubrics, that is, your performance will be evaluated from aspects:

- Organization
- Delivery manners
- Content
- Graph Description

## Samples: Rubrics for Evaluating Your Research Report

### Organization (1)

| Name | Their Way to Get Attention | | | Are the Presenters Audience-Friendly? | | | Is Their Presentation Complete? | | | The Average Score |
|---|---|---|---|---|---|---|---|---|---|---|
| | good | ok | poor | good | ok | poor | good | ok | poor | |
| | 4 – 5ps | 2 – 3ps | 1p | 4 – 5ps | 2 – 3ps | 1p | 4 – 5ps | 2 – 3ps | 1p | |
| | | | | | | | | | | |

### Organization (2)

| Name | Their Way to Introduce Topic/Main Idea | | | Their Use of Transitions | | | Their Way to Finish off the Presentation | | | The Average Score |
|---|---|---|---|---|---|---|---|---|---|---|
| | good | ok | poor | good | ok | poor | good | ok | poor | |
| | 4 – 5ps | 2 – 3ps | 1p | 4 – 5ps | 2 – 3ps | 1p | 4 – 5ps | 2 – 3ps | 1p | |
| | | | | | | | | | | |

## Delivery manners (1)

| Name | Speed | | | Sound Volume | | | Pronunciation | | | Using Visual Aids | | | The Average Score |
|---|---|---|---|---|---|---|---|---|---|---|---|---|---|
| | good | ok | poor | good | ok | poor | good | ok | poor | good | ok | poor | |
| | 4 – 5ps | 2 – 3ps | 1p | 4 – 5ps | 2 – 3ps | 1p | 4 – 5ps | 2 – 3ps | 1p | 4 – 5ps | 2 – 3ps | 1p | |
| | | | | | | | | | | | | | |

## Delivery manners (2)

| Name | Staging/Positioning | | | Body Language (Including Using Pointer) | | | Using Pauses | | | The Average Score |
|---|---|---|---|---|---|---|---|---|---|---|
| | good | ok | poor | good | ok | poor | good | ok | poor | |
| | 4 – 5ps | 2 – 3ps | 1p | 4 – 5ps | 2 – 3ps | 1p | 4 – 5ps | 2 – 3ps | 1p | |
| | | | | | | | | | | |

## Content

| Name | Purpose of research | | | Research Methods | | | Research Results | | | Findings of Research | | | The Average Score |
|---|---|---|---|---|---|---|---|---|---|---|---|---|---|
| | good | ok | poor | good | ok | poor | good | ok | poor | good | ok | poor | |
| | 4 – 5ps | 2 – 3ps | 1p | 4 – 5ps | 2 – 3ps | 1p | 4 – 5ps | 2 – 3ps | 1p | 4 – 5ps | 2 – 3ps | 1p | |
| | | | | | | | | | | | | | |

## Graph Description

| Name | Good | Need Improved | Poor |
|---|---|---|---|
| | 4. 5 – 5 | 3 – 4 | 0 – 2. 5 |
| | | | |

# 2

CAMPING

**Public Forum Debate
Camping**

CAMPING

- PFD Knowledge Base
- PFD Skills Camp
- PFD Practice Camp

## Project 1
## PFD Knowledge Base

◈ Task: Understanding what public forum debate is

➲ **Step 1**   Read **References 1** and do annotated reading to understand what Public Forum Debate (PFD) is.

➲ **Step 2**   Compose a topic outline of "101: Introduction to PDF" in **Reference 1**.

# Poject 2
# PFD Skills Training Camp

## ◈ Task 1: Learning to construct a case

| Motion: All courses should be optional.<br>Affirmative/Proposition side: Group 1/3/5/...<br>Negative/Opposition side: Group 2/4/6/... | | |
|---|---|---|
| Steps | Jobs | Reminders |
| Step 1 | 1. Before class, do annotated reading of "The Case: Constructive", "Constructing Case" and "Mastering Constructives" in Reference 1.<br>2. According to your reading, make a checklist of jobs for constructing a case. | ☺ This is an individual job. |
| Step 2 | 3. The whole class will be divided into even-numbered groups. Two groups will work together later. | ☺ The recommended number of people per group is 3 or 4. |
| Step 3 | 4. Work in your groups.<br>• Discuss your checklist of jobs for constructing a case.<br>• Prepare for the debate on the motion given. The focus skill for this practice is constructing a case and doing constructive speech. Use the checklist while you are working in this period.<br>• Discuss sub-claims and evidence the opposite side may use and figure out how to do rebuttal.<br>• Decide your roles in the debate.<br>• Prepare your own job in the debate, including the expressions for debate. | ☺ This group work will last 40 min.<br>☺ Use brainstorming and decide the sub-claims/contentions and evidence to support your position or to refute your opposite side.<br>☺ Use Toulmin Model when necessary. |

| | |
|---|---|
| Step 4 | 5. Two groups work together and conduct the debate.<br><br>G1＋G2<br>G3＋G4<br>G5＋G6<br>G...＋G...<br><br>**Proposition #1**<br>(1st debater)<br>opening, definition, teamline, constructing own case<br>⇨<br>**Opposition #1**<br>(1st debater)<br>accepting definition/redefinition, teamline, constructing own case<br><br>**Proposition #2**<br>(2nd debater)<br>rebuttal of 1st Opp., rebuild own case<br>⇨<br>**Opposition #2**<br>(2nd debater)<br>rebuttal of 2nd Prop., rebuild own case<br><br>**Proposition #3**<br>(3rd debater)<br>general rebuttal, rebuild own case<br>⇨<br>**Opposition #3**<br>(3rd debater)<br>general rebuttal, rebuild own case<br><br>**Proposition #4**<br>(3−member Groups: 1st/2nd speaker;<br>4−member Groups: 4th speaker<br>reply, summary, ending)<br>⇦<br>**Opposition #4**<br>(3−member Groups: 1st/2nd speaker;<br>4−member Groups: 4th speaker<br>summary, ending) |

| | | |
|---|---|---|
| Step 5 | 6. After class, write down your own case based on your debate. | ☺ Write this work according to what you have learned from Reference 1.<br>☺ Hand in your work to your teacher before the deadline. |

## ◈ Task 2: Learning to do rebuttal by using different ways of argument

| Motion: Renewable energy should replace fossil fuels. | | |
|---|---|---|
| Steps | Jobs | Reminders |
| Step 1 | 1. The whole class will be divided into 2 teams: affirmative side and negative side.<br>2. Before the class, do the individual jobs:<br>• Search more evidence to support your position;<br>• Figure out three outlines based on the 3 ways of argument;<br>• Bring your outlines to this Wednesday's class. | ☺ The division should be assigned at the end of the last class. |
| Step 2 | 3. Take a seat. Positive side take the seats out the circle; negative, inside.<br><br>Teacher's Desk<br><br>4. Find 2 or 3 persons except your neighbors who have the same position with you and share your argument outlines with them. Take notes and improve your outlines. (20 min) | |
| Step 3 | 5. Be ready to give an individual presentation according to your outlines.<br>• Those who take the positive side will give an oral presentation by using classical argument.<br>• Those who take the negative side will give an oral presentation by using Toulmin argument. | ☺ Time for each presentation: 3 – 4 min<br>☺ Use the proper expressions to express your arguments. |

| | | |
|---|---|---|
| Step 4 | 6. Two positions stand one by one face to face. Remember your number.<br><br>7. Proposition ♯ 1/3/5/7/9/11/13/15 stand up and do your presentation. (4 min)<br><br>8. Opposition ♯ 1/3/5/7/9/11/13/15 stand up and do your presentation. (4 min)<br><br>9. Proposition ♯ 2/4/6/8/10/12/14 stand up and do your presentation. (4 min)<br><br>10. Opposition ♯ 2/4/6/8/10/12/14 stand up and do your presentation. (4 min)<br><br>11. Two teams try to convince the other side by using Rogerian argument person to person. (4 min×2)<br><br>12. Negative side moves to the next opposite partner and do your persuasion with Rogerian argument again. (3 min×2)<br><br>13. Negative side moves to the next opposite partner and do your persuasion with Rogerian argument again. (2 min×2) | ☺ There will be a 5‑minute preparation time between steps 4 and 5.<br><br>☺ Take notes while you are listening to your neighbors' presentations. |

## ◈ Task 3: Learning to do a crossfire

The whole class will be divided into 9 groups.

| Motion: Who can be the coach of the national male football team? Cao Cao or Liu Bei |||
|---|---|---|
| • Affirmative/Proposition side: Group 1/3/5/7/9 (Cao Cao) |||
| • Negative/Opposition side: Group 2/4/6/8 (Liu Bei) |||

| Steps | Jobs | Reminders |
|---|---|---|
| Step 1 | 1. Read References 2, 3, 4, and take notes. (40 min) | ☺ This is an individual job.<br>☺ The notes can be the answers to the questions:<br>• What is the purpose of crossfire?<br>• What do you need to accomplish during crossfire?<br>• What strategies can you use to accomplish your goals in crossfire?<br>• What types of questions can we use?<br>• What are the uses of the different types of questions for cross-examination?<br>☺ The notes can be other important information about crossfire. |
| Step 2 | 2. Work in your group and orally share the notes in turns. Each turn will be about 2 minutes. (15 – 20 min) | |

| | | |
|---|---|---|
| Step 3 | 3. Construct your case.<br>• Have a discussion about the 3 questions. (15 min)<br>*Type of claim?*<br>*How to develop the argument of your position?*<br>*How to build up the opening statement?*<br>• After the discussion, every memberrehearses the 4 – minute constructive speech. (10 min) | |
| Step 4 | 4. Three groups work together and be ready to have a debate.<br><br>Group 1 (A)<br>Group 2 (N)  Team 1  Group 3 (A)<br><br>Group 4 (N)<br>Group 5 (A)  Team 2  Group 6 (N)<br><br>Group 7 (A)<br>Group 8 (N)  Team 3  Group 9 (A)<br><br>Take notes for your crossfire!!!<br>4 min×3<br>5. Select one in your group to present the constructive presentation. | |
| Step 5 | 6. Work in your group and design the questions for crossfire.<br>7. Practice asking the questions before you do the crossfire with your opposite side. | ☺ Time limit: 20 min |

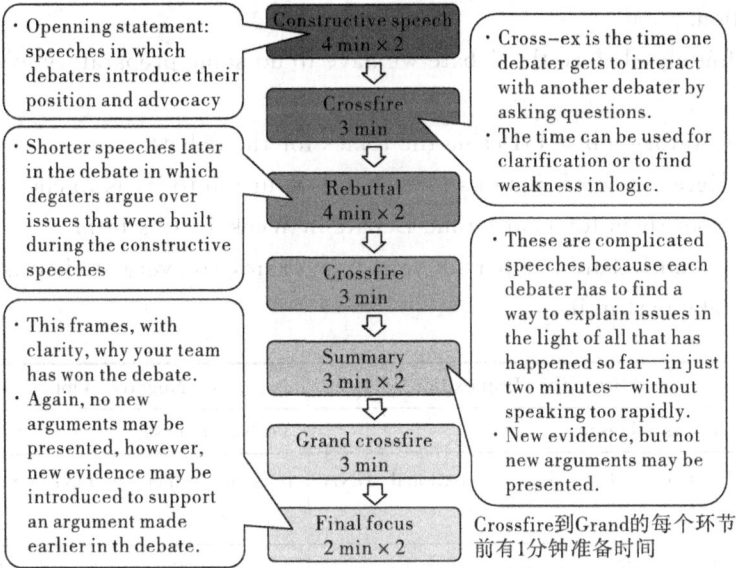

| | |
|---|---|
| Step 6 | 8. Work in your team again. One group will be the judge group appointed by your teacher and meanwhile they will be the chairperson and timekeepers.<br><br>9. The other two groups will have a debate by using the following flow. Assign your roles in the Debate.<br><br>＊Remember: the focus of this practice is asking and answering questions in crossfire.<br><br>· Openning statement: speeches in which debaters introduce their position and advocacy<br><br>Constructive speech 4 min × 2<br><br>· Cross−ex is the time one debater gets to interact with another debater by asking questions.<br>· The time can be used for clarification or to find weakness in logic.<br><br>Crossfire 3 min<br><br>· Shorter speeches later in the debate in which degaters argue over issues that were built during the constructive speeches<br><br>Rebuttal 4 min × 2<br><br>Crossfire 3 min<br><br>· These are complicated speeches because each debater has to find a way to explain issues in the light of all that has happened so far—in just two minutes—without speaking too rapidly.<br>· New evidence, but not new arguments may be presented.<br><br>· This frames, with clarity, why your team has won the debate.<br>· Again, no new arguments may be presented, however, new evidence may be introduced to support an argument made earlier in th debate.<br><br>Summary 3 min × 2<br><br>Grand crossfire 3 min<br><br>Final focus 2 min × 2<br><br>Crossfire到Grand的每个环节前有1分钟准备时间<br><br>10. Have your debate. Shoulder your responsibility! |
| Step 7 | 11. When the debate is finished, the judge groups will give comments on the performance of the two groups in the debate and the quality of asking and answering the questions. |

◈ Task：Conducting grand debate

We are going to have a whole-grade debate named Grand Debate. For the detailed arrangement and grouping for the debate，please follow your teacher's instruction.

Definitely，before the debate we have to do some preparatory jobs.

Preparatory job ＃1：Decide the topics for the debate.
- Here are some motions for debate. Your job today is to choose 8 motions from them for your Grand Debate in Week 16 this term.
- Grand Debate is a part of your final exam，so every student is required to take part in it.

| No. | Affirmative/Proposition | Negative/Opposition |
|---|---|---|
| 1 | Tech is a blessing. | Tech is a curse. |
| 2 | It is ethical to have a national DNA database. | It is not ethical to have a national DNA database. |
| 3 | All scientific research should be made open access. | All scientific research should be made open access. |
| 4 | Artificial intelligence is dangerous. | Artificial intelligence is not dangerous. |
| 5 | Online learning vs. traditional learning. Which is better? (online learning) | Online learning vs. traditional learning. Which is better? (traditional learning) |
| 6 | Vegetarianism is the solution to the environmental crisis. | Vegetarianism is not the solution to the environmental crisis. |
| 7 | Competition is more important than cooperation in the learning process. | Cooperation is more important than competition in the learning process. |
| 8 | Ability is more important than opportunity for one's success. | Opportunity is more important than ability for one's success. |
| 9 | Selfishness in a disaster should be blamed. | Selfishness in a disaster should not be blamed. |

(Continued)

| No. | Affirmative/Proposition | Negative/Opposition |
|---|---|---|
| 10 | The popularity of short video is the embodiment of cultural prosperity. | The popularity of short video is the manifestation of cultural scarcity. |
| 11 | The more you know, the happier you are. | The less you know, the happier you are. |
| 12 | The Internet is making it harder for us to know the truth. | The Internet is making it easier for us to know the truth. |

☺ How to do it?

Group work (30 min):

- Discuss some criteria for selecting a proper motion for a debate and submit your criteria to our **QQ** group. (10 min)
- Select 8 out of 13 motions according to your criteria. (20 min)
- Hand in your discussion results to our **QQ** group when the time is up.

Preparatory job ♯ 2: Work with your partners to do the preparation according to what you have learned from **References 1** to **5**.

## References

1. https://www.debatedrills.com/public-forum/what-is-public-forum
2. https://www.wcdebate.com/2ld/7cx.htm
3. https://www.mustangps.org/Downloads/Chapter％20VIII％20-％20 Questioning％20and％20Crossfire.pdf
4. https://www.debateresource.com/post/what-questions-should-i-ask-to-win-crossfire
5. https://pfdebate.info/getting-started/